This book belongs to:

_____

© Copyright 2021-2025- All rights reserved.

You may not reproduce, duplicate or send the contents of this book without direct written permission from the author. You cannot hereby despite any circumstance blame the publisher or hold him or her to legal responsibility for any reparation, compensations, or monetary forfeiture owing to the information included herein, either in a direct or an indirect way.

Legal Notice: This book has copyright protection. You can use the book for personal purpose. You should not sell, use, alter, distribute, quote, take excerpts or paraphrase in part or whole the material contained in this book without obtaining the permission of the author first.

Disclaimer Notice: You must take note that the information in this document is for casual reading and entertainment purposes only. We have made every attempt to provide accurate, up to date and reliable information. We do not express or imply guarantees of any kind. The persons who read admit that the writer is not occupied in giving legal, financial, medical or other advice. We put this book content by sourcing various places.

Please consult a licensed professional before you try any techniques shown in this book. By going through this document, the book lover comes to an agreement that under no situation is the author accountable for any forfeiture, direct or indirect, which they may incur because of the use of material contained in this document, including, but not limited to, —errors, omissions, or inaccuracies.

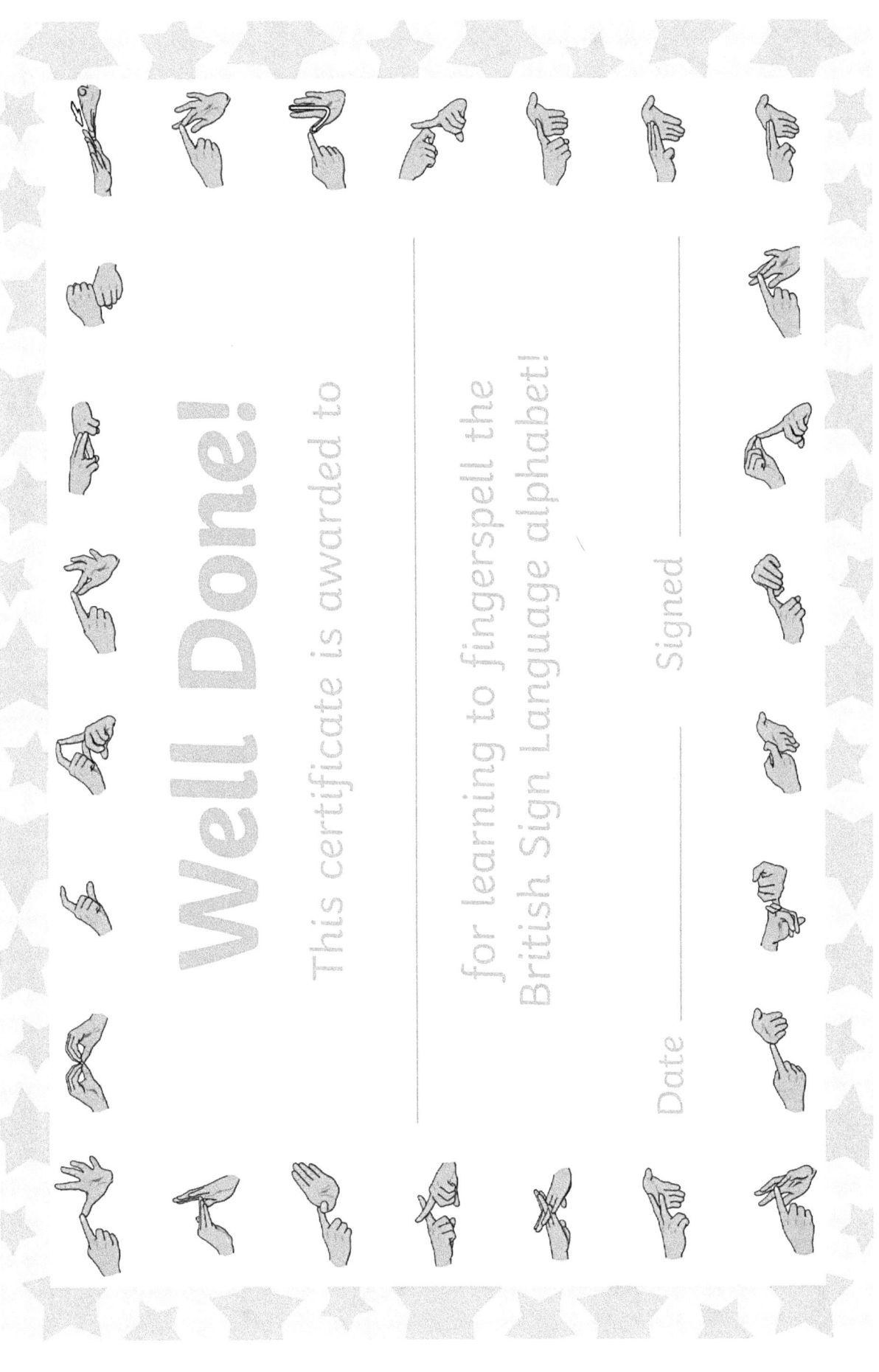

apple

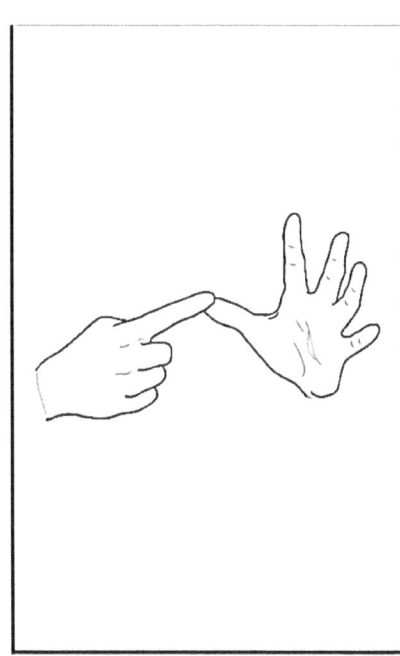

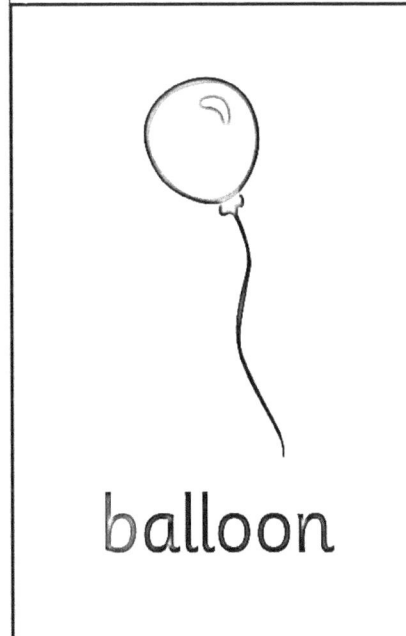

balloon

  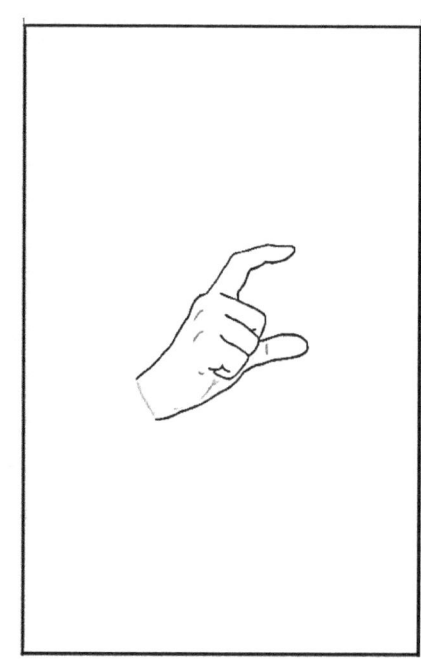

cat

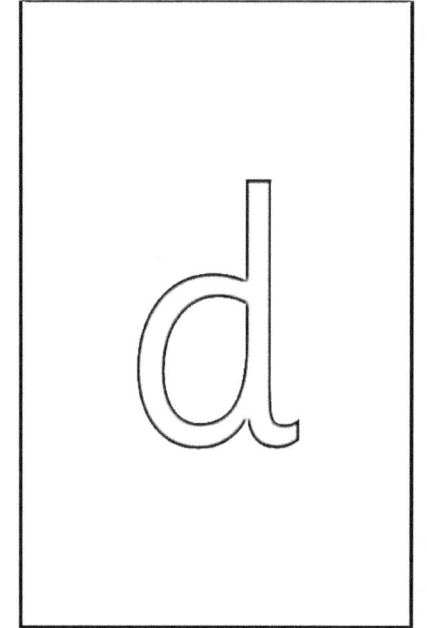  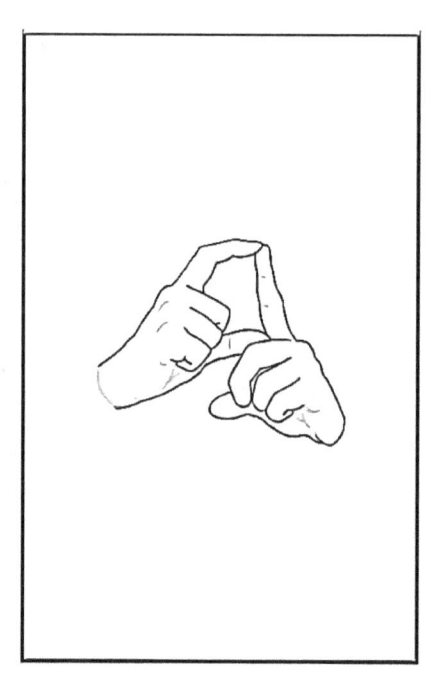

dog

  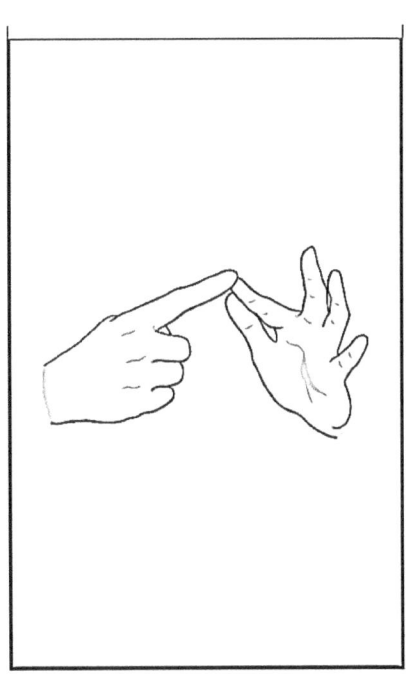

elephant

  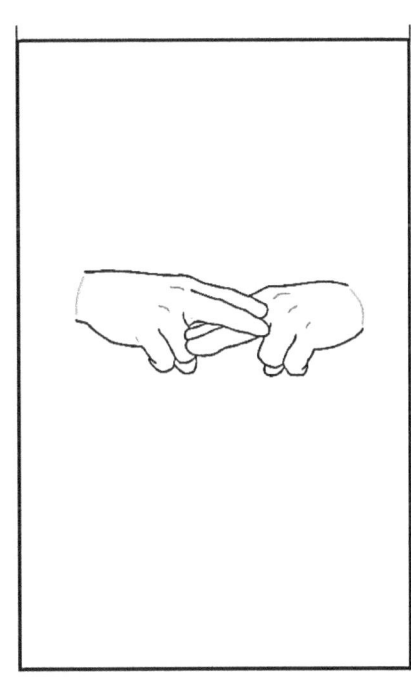

frog

goat

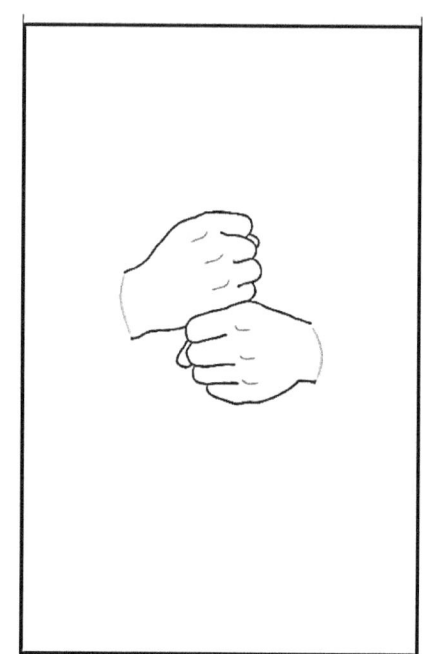

hat

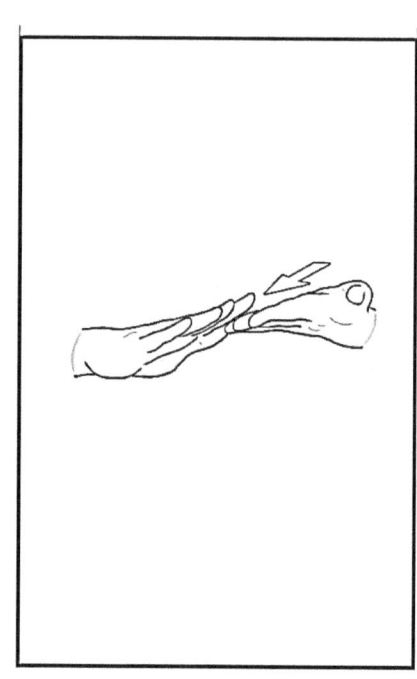

ink

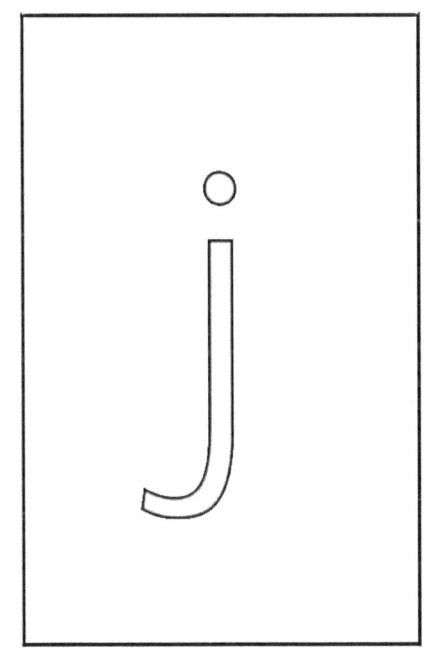  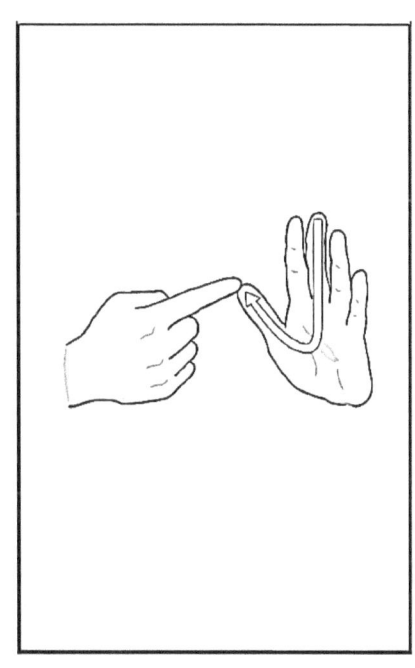

jumper

  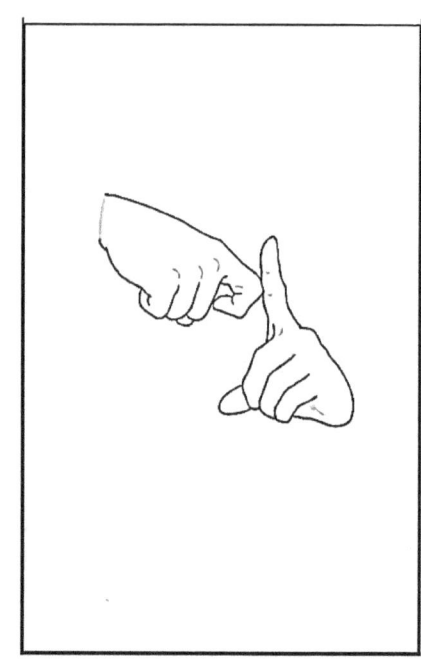

kite

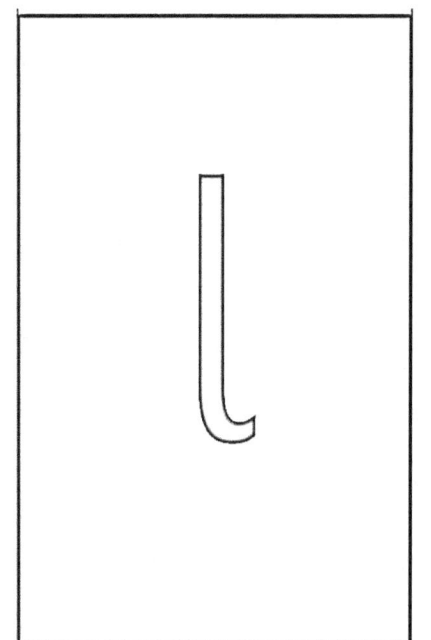  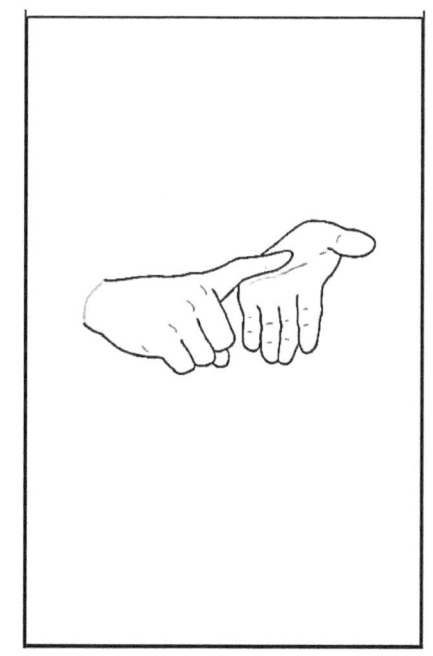

leaf

  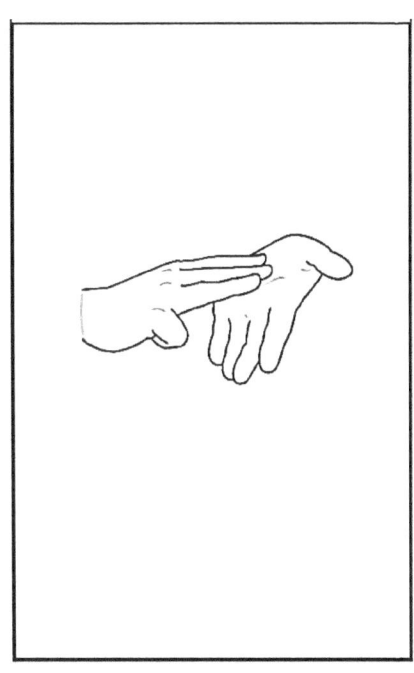

monkey

 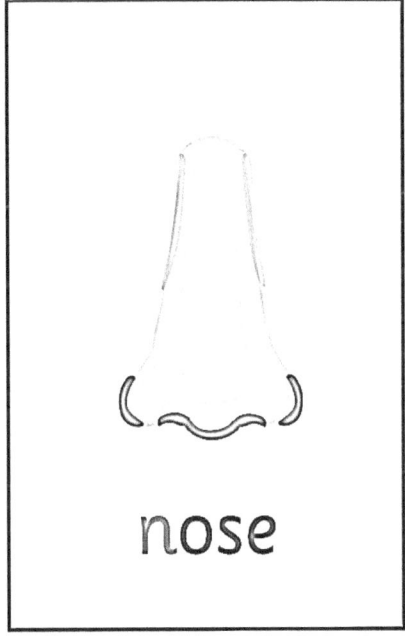 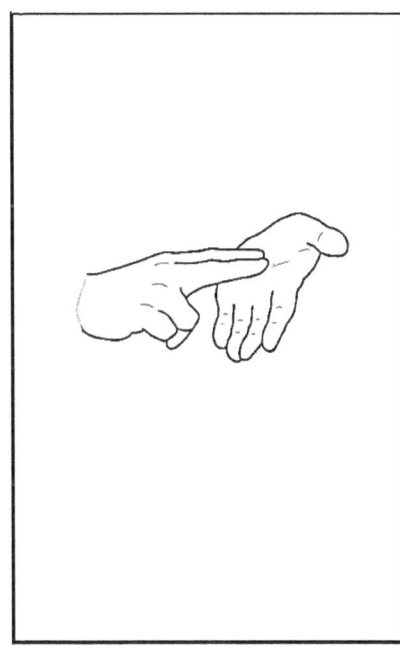

nose

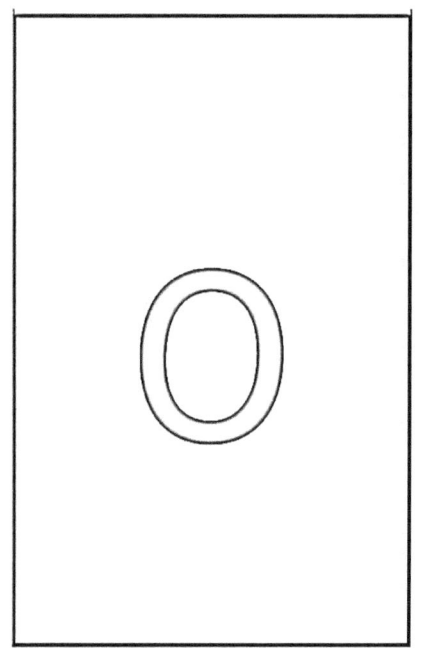

octopus

parrot
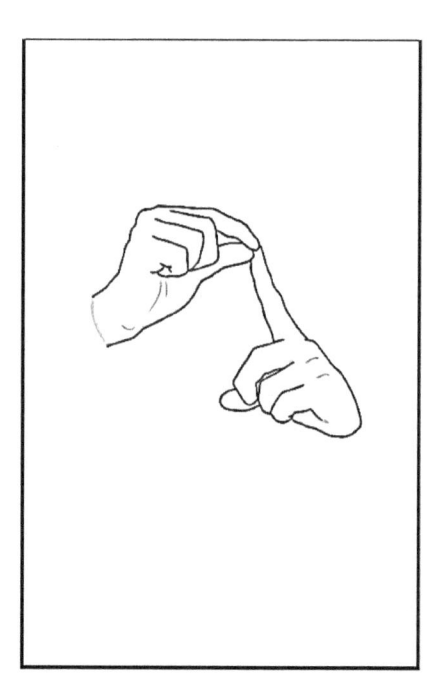

queen
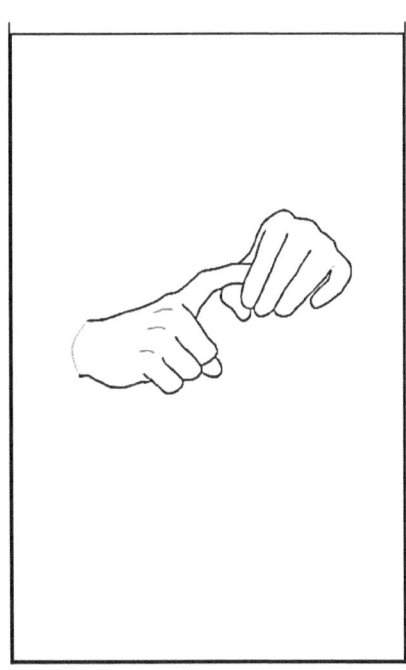

robot
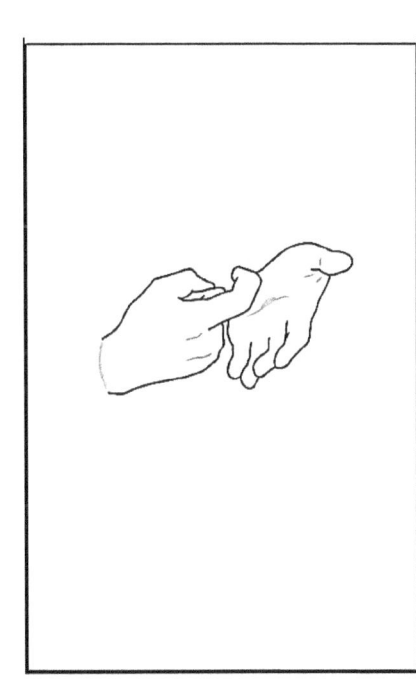

S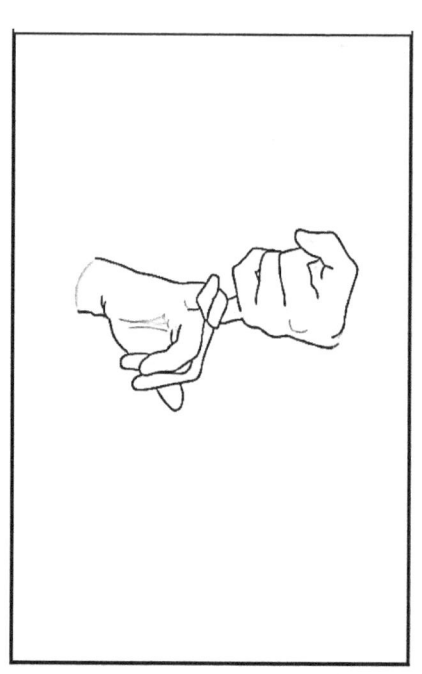

submarine

t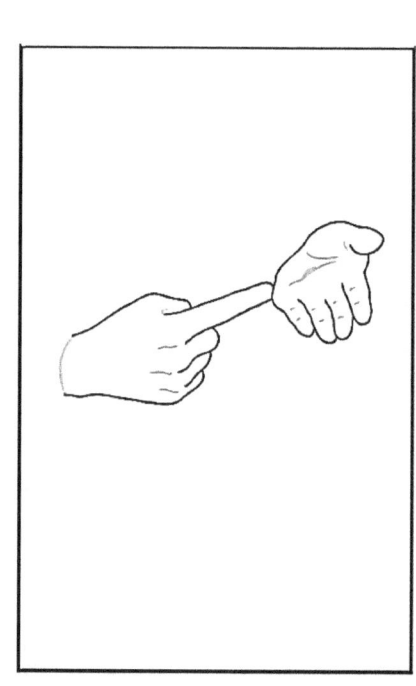

turtle

umbrella

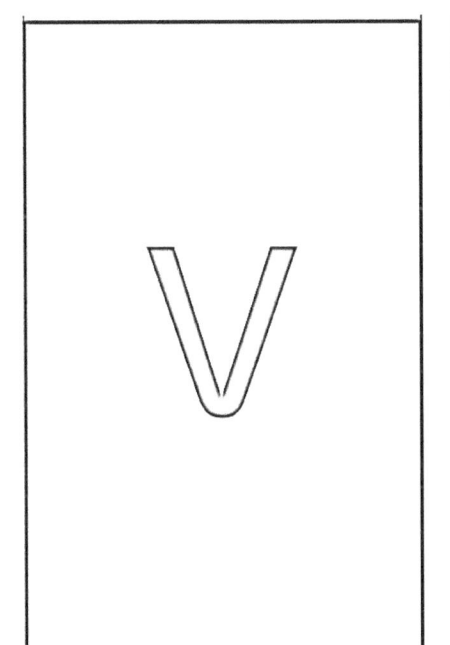  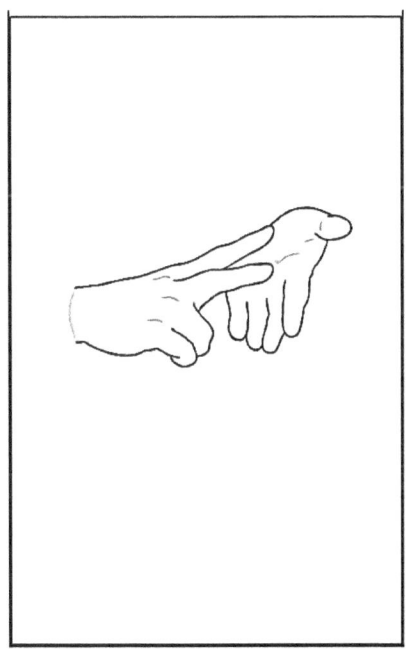

volcano

watch

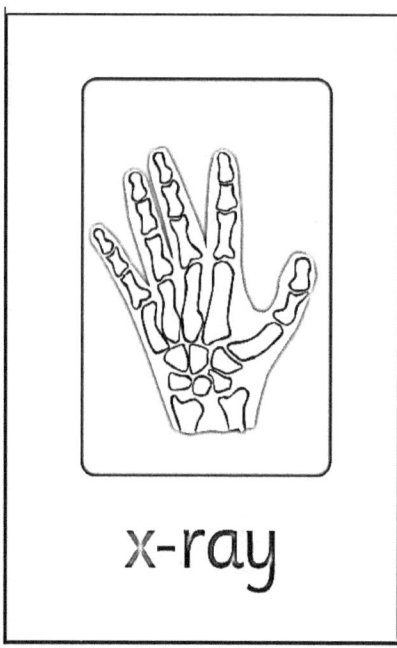
x-ray
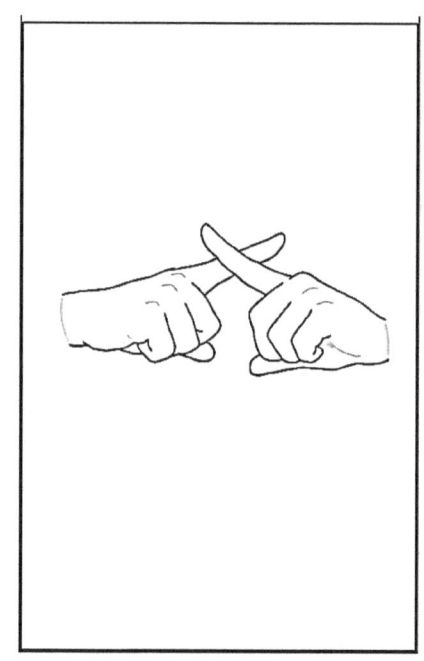

yoghurt
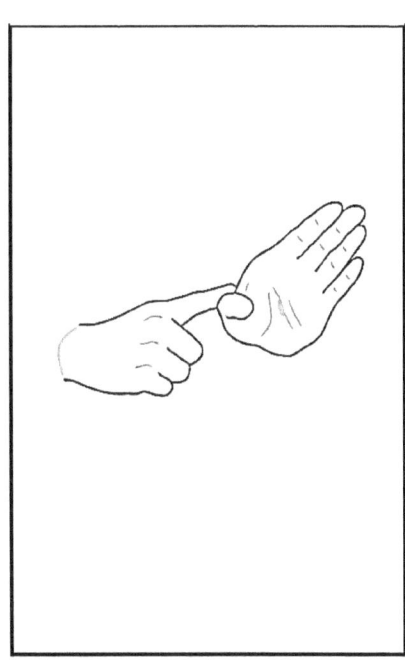

zebra

Pick the correct fingerspelling sign to complete the word.

Pick the correct fingerspelling sign to complete the word.

British Sign Language Fingerspelling Colour Maze - A

Help the girl get to the apple by colouring all the 'a' fingerspelling signs.

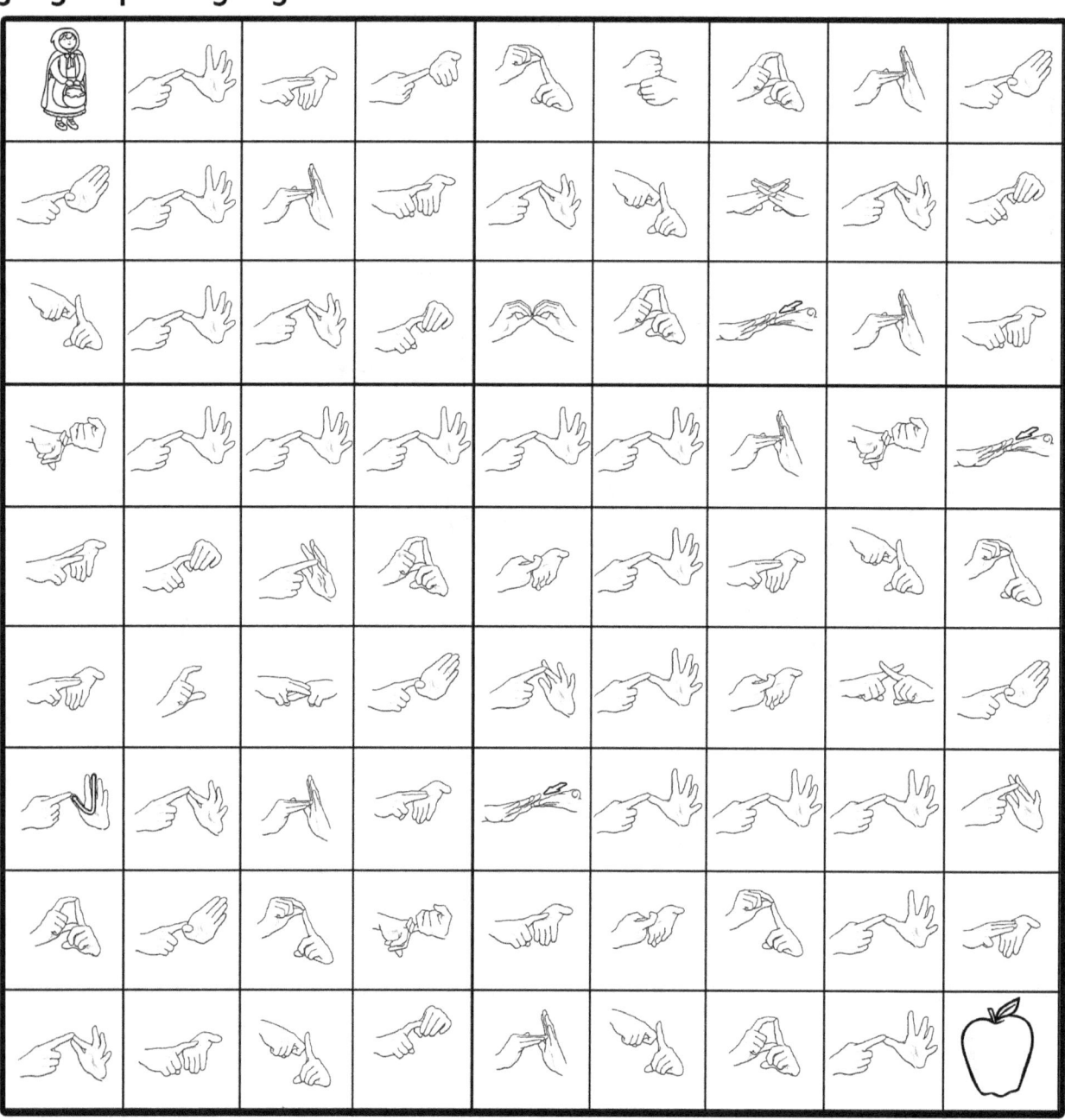

British Sign Language Fingerspelling Colour Maze - E

Help the elephant get to the peanut butter by colouring all the 'e' fingerspelling signs.

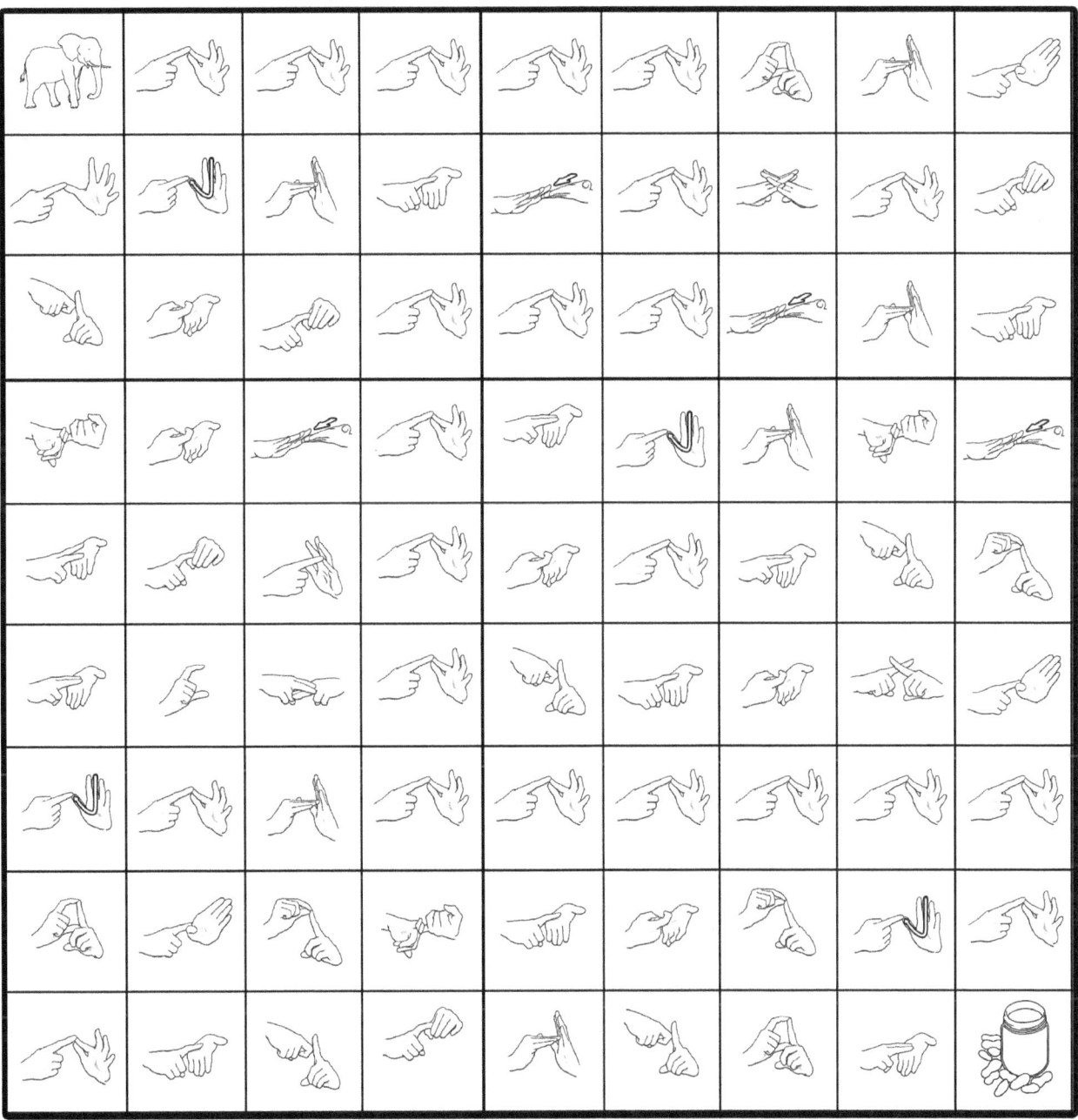

British Sign Language Fingerspelling Colour Maze - I

Help get the pen get to the ink by colouring all the 'i' fingerspelling signs.

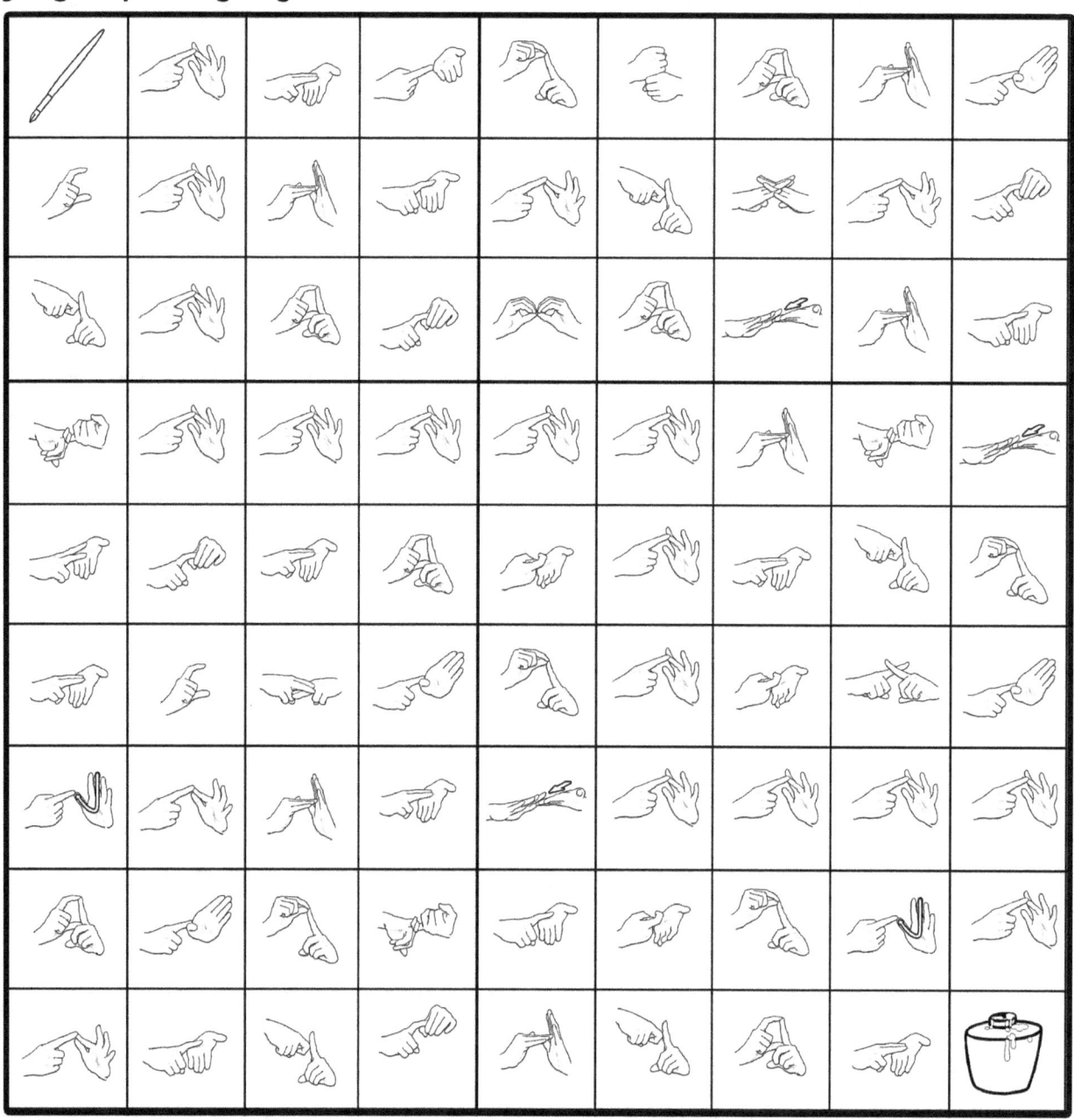

British Sign Language Fingerspelling Colour Maze - O

Help the octopus get to the shipwreck by colouring all the 'o' fingerspelling signs.

British Sign Language Fingerspelling Colour Maze - U

Help get the umbrella to the children by colouring all the 'u' fingerspelling signs.

FINGERSPELLING

apple
school
teacher
pupil

class
lesson
learn
pencil

Fingerspelling Answers

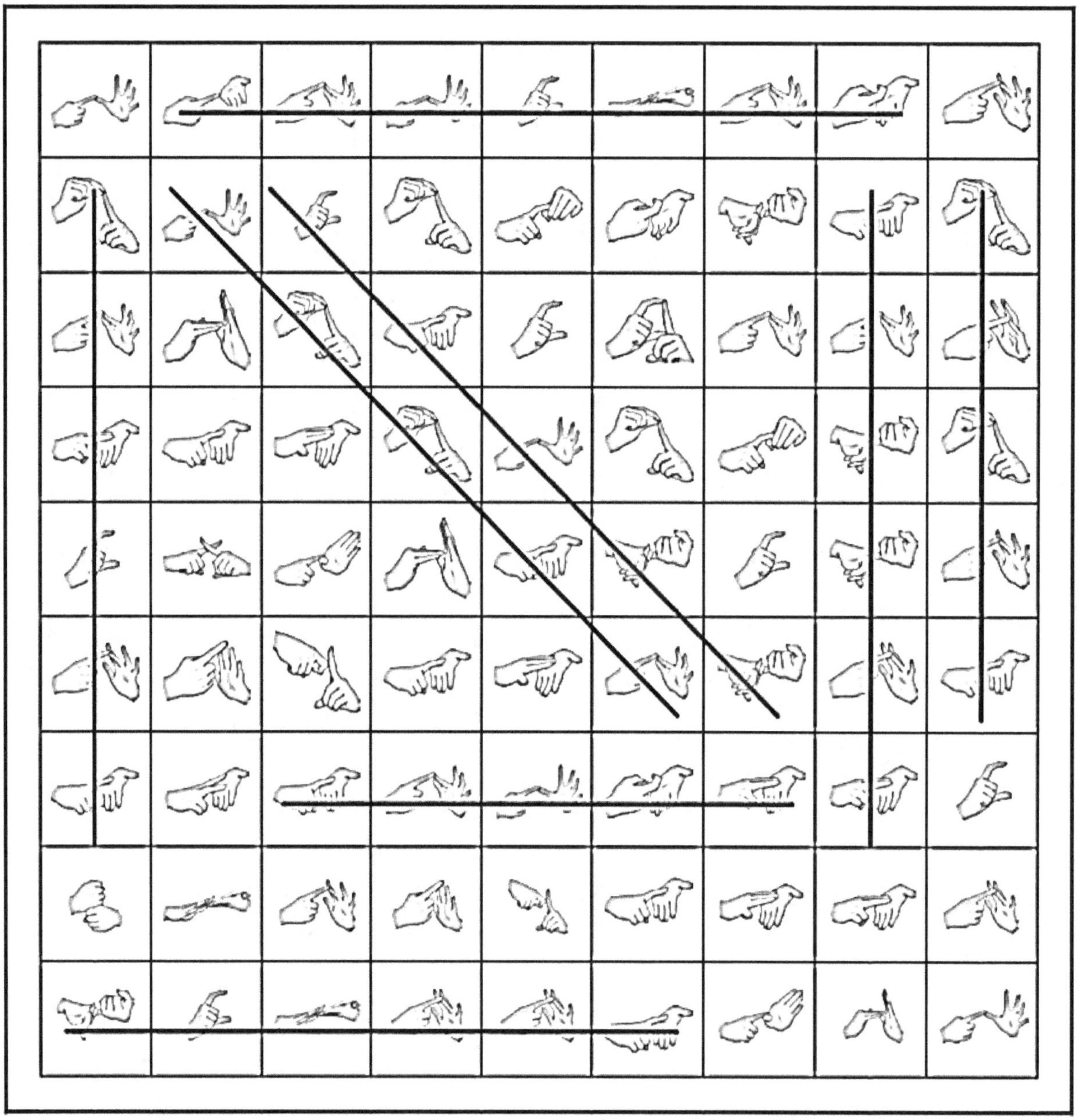

apple   class
school   lesson
teacher   learn
pupil   pencil

0
1
2
3
4
5
6
7
8
9
10
11
12
13
14
15
16
17

18
19
20

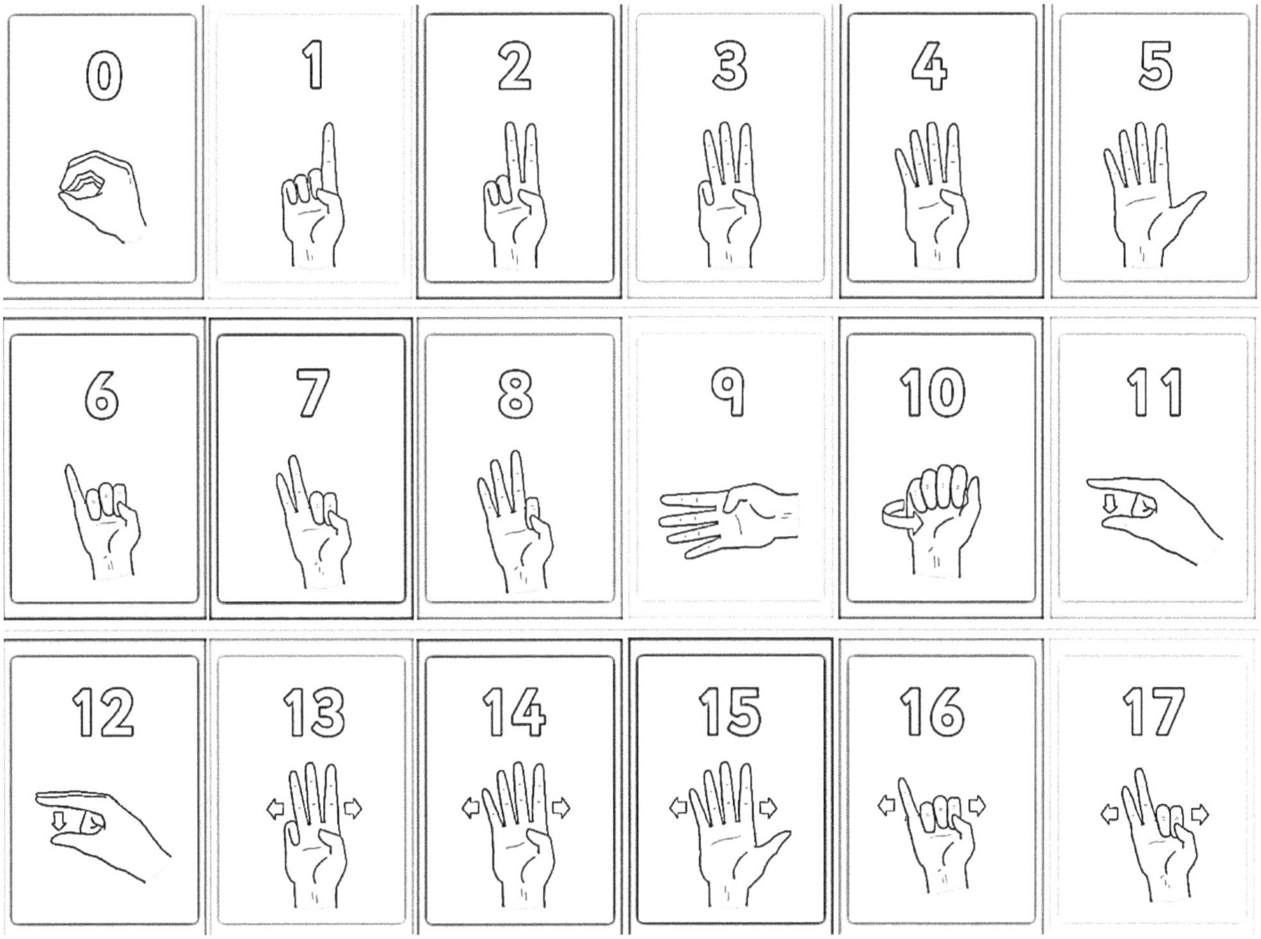

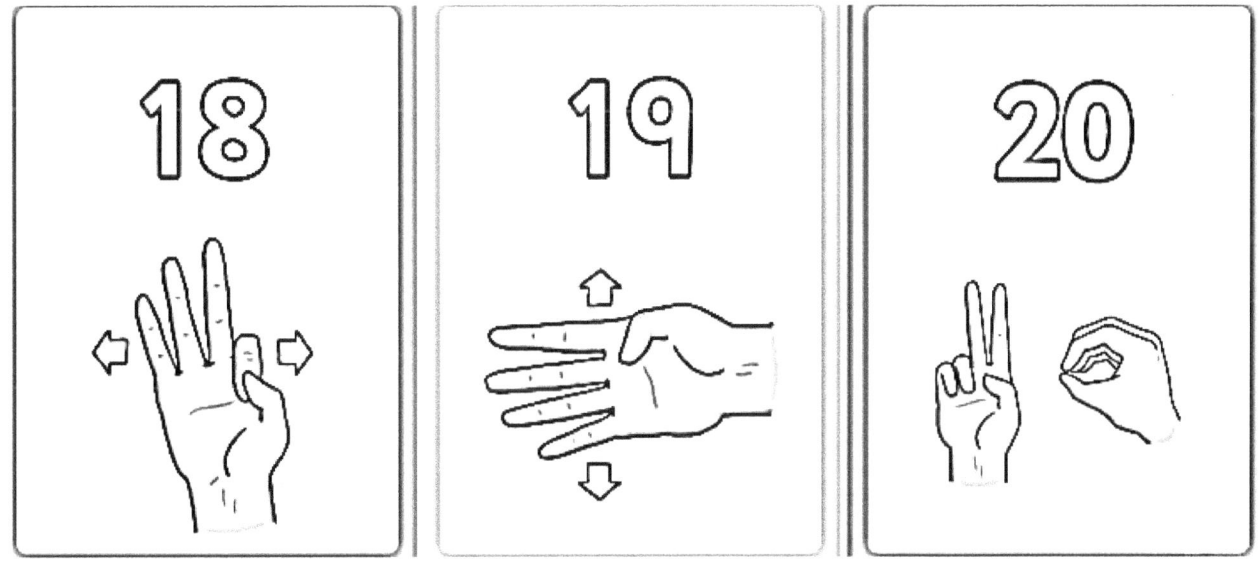

Missing BSL Number Challenge Cards

Missing Number

1.

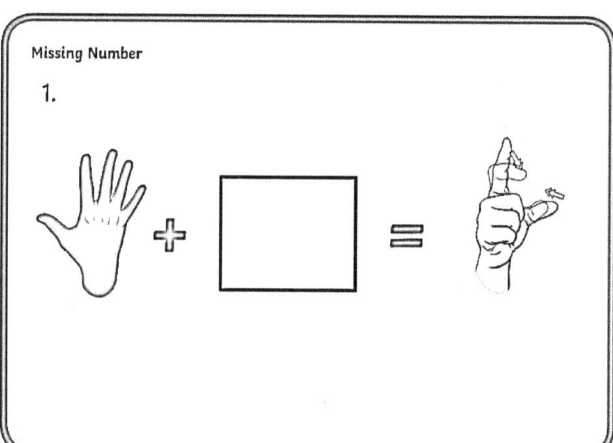

Missing Number

2.

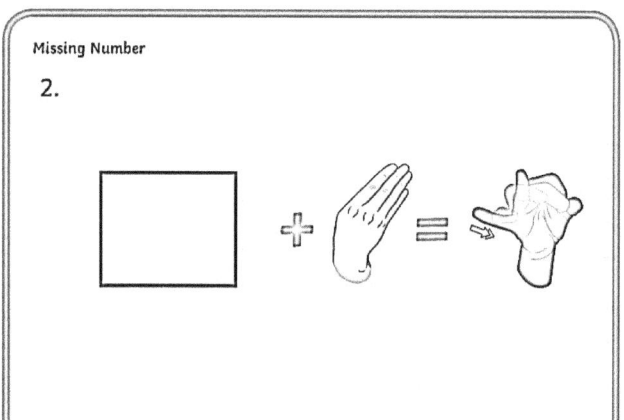

Missing Number

3.

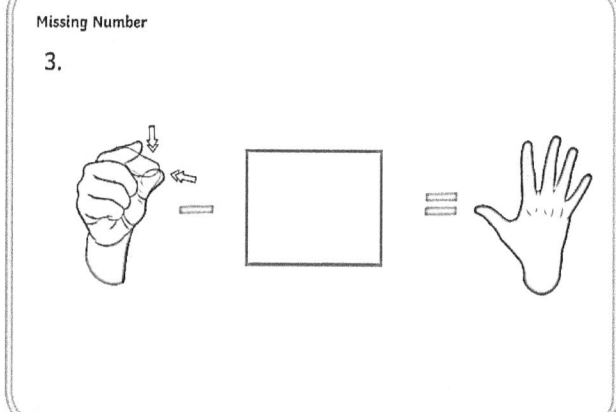

Missing Number

4.

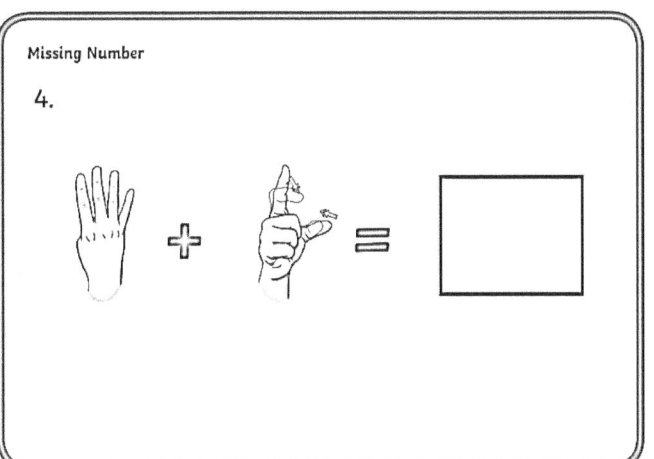

Missing Number

5.

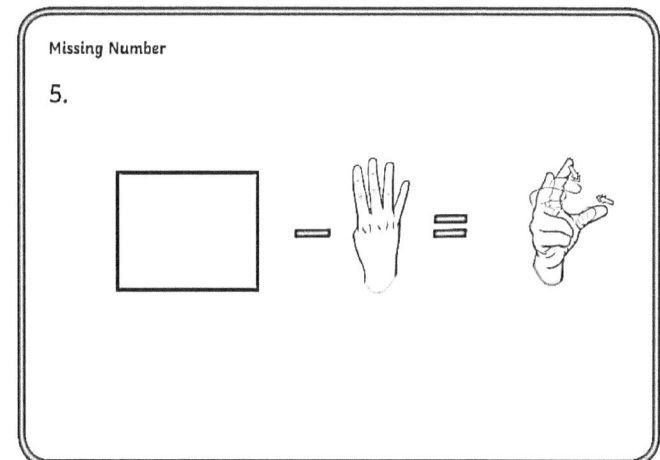

Missing Number

6.

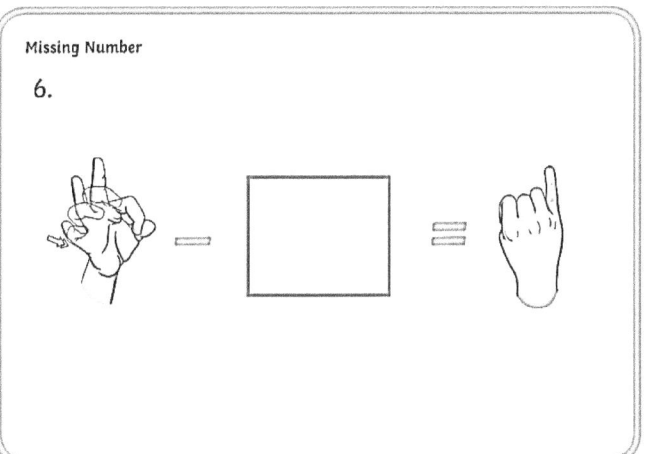

Missing Number

7.

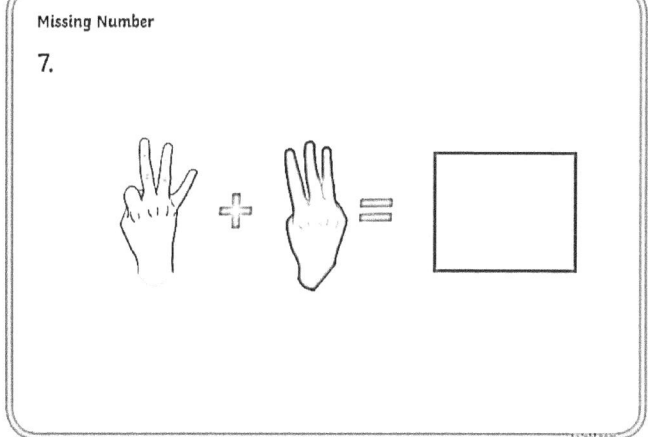

Missing Number

8.

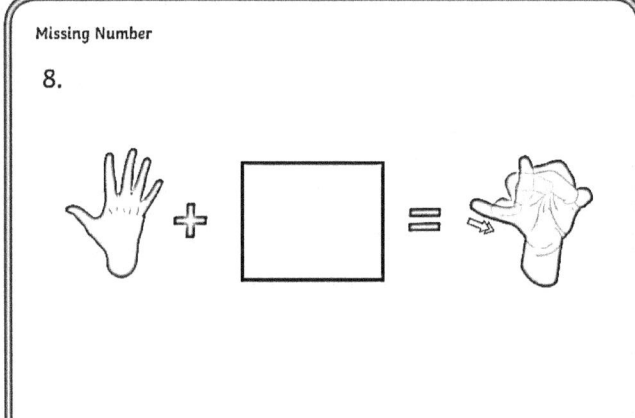

9.

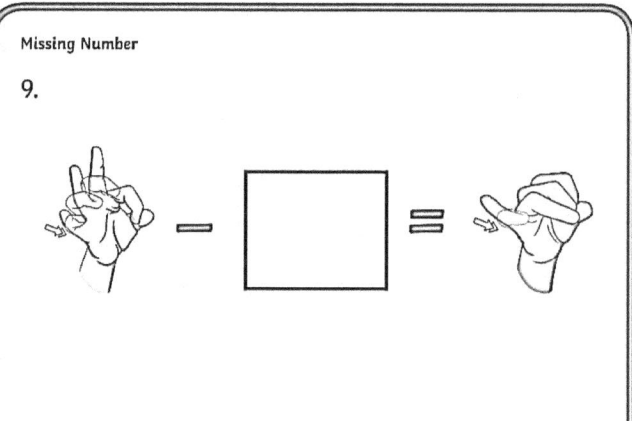

10.

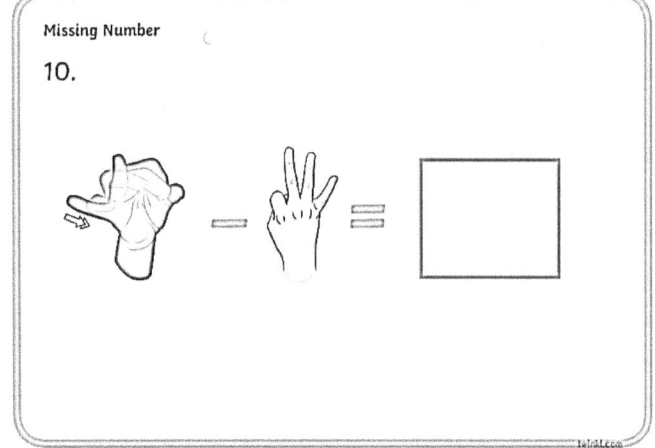

11.

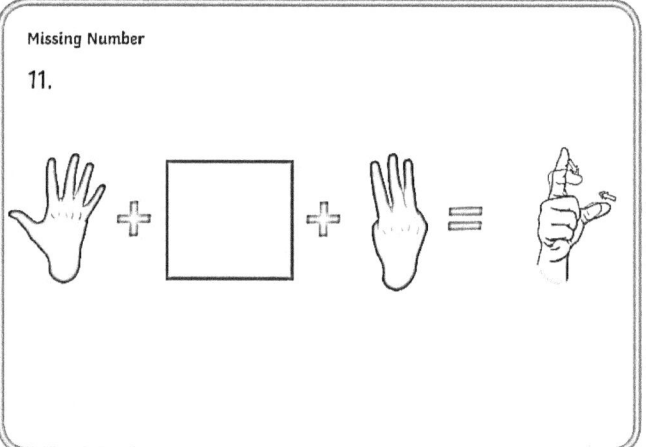

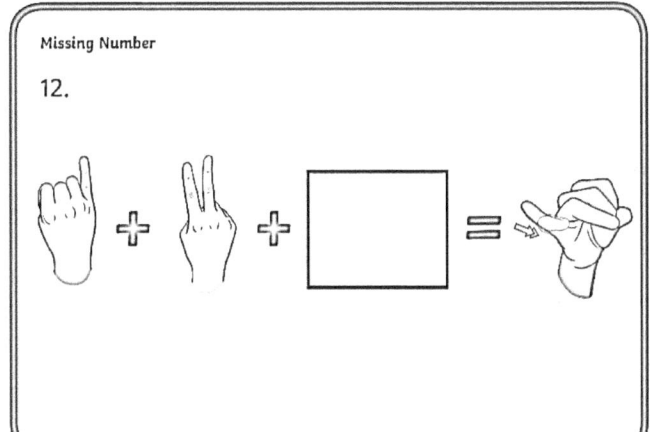

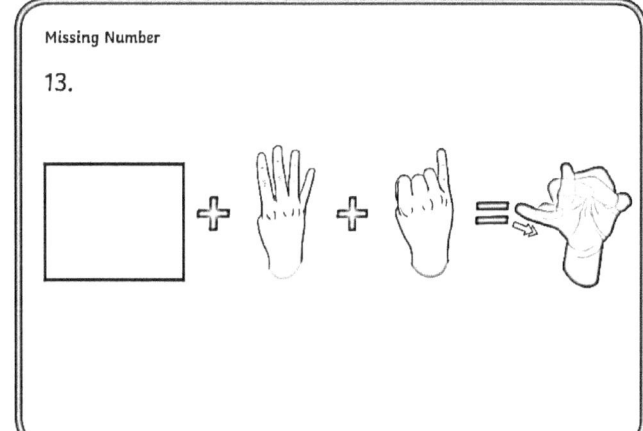

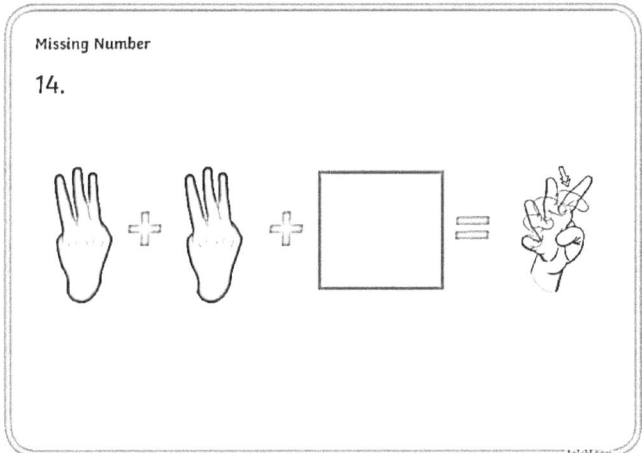

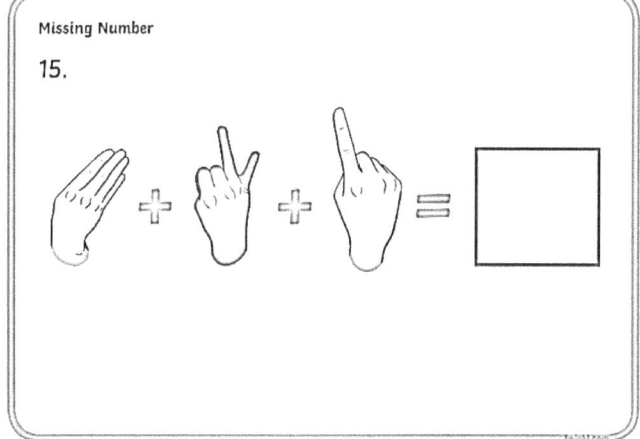

Missing Number

Answers

1. 7
2. 8
3. 15
4. 20
5. 17
6. 12
7. 11
8. 12
9. 2
10. 9
11. 4
12. 8
13. 7
14. 8
15. 17

British Sign Language Alphabet Sign and Letter Matching

Draw a line from each sign to the matching letter.

A

V

X

H

K

P

D

J

British Sign Language Alphabet Sign and Letter Matching

Draw a line from each sign to the matching letter.

T

U

Q

O

E

M

G

W

N

British Sign Language Alphabet Sign and Letter Matching

Draw a line from each sign to the matching letter.

R

S

I

B

Z

L

Y

C

F

Monday

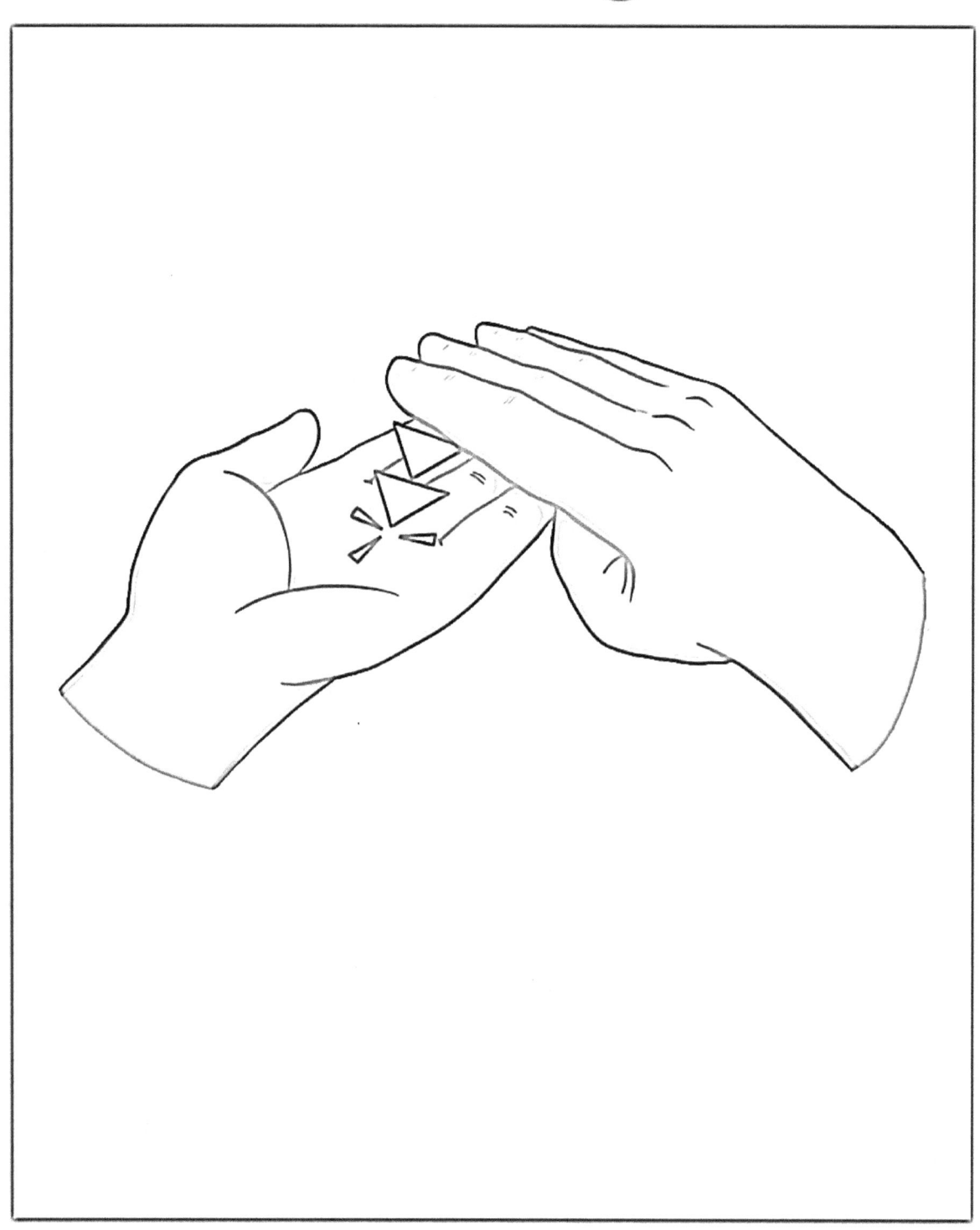

Tuesday

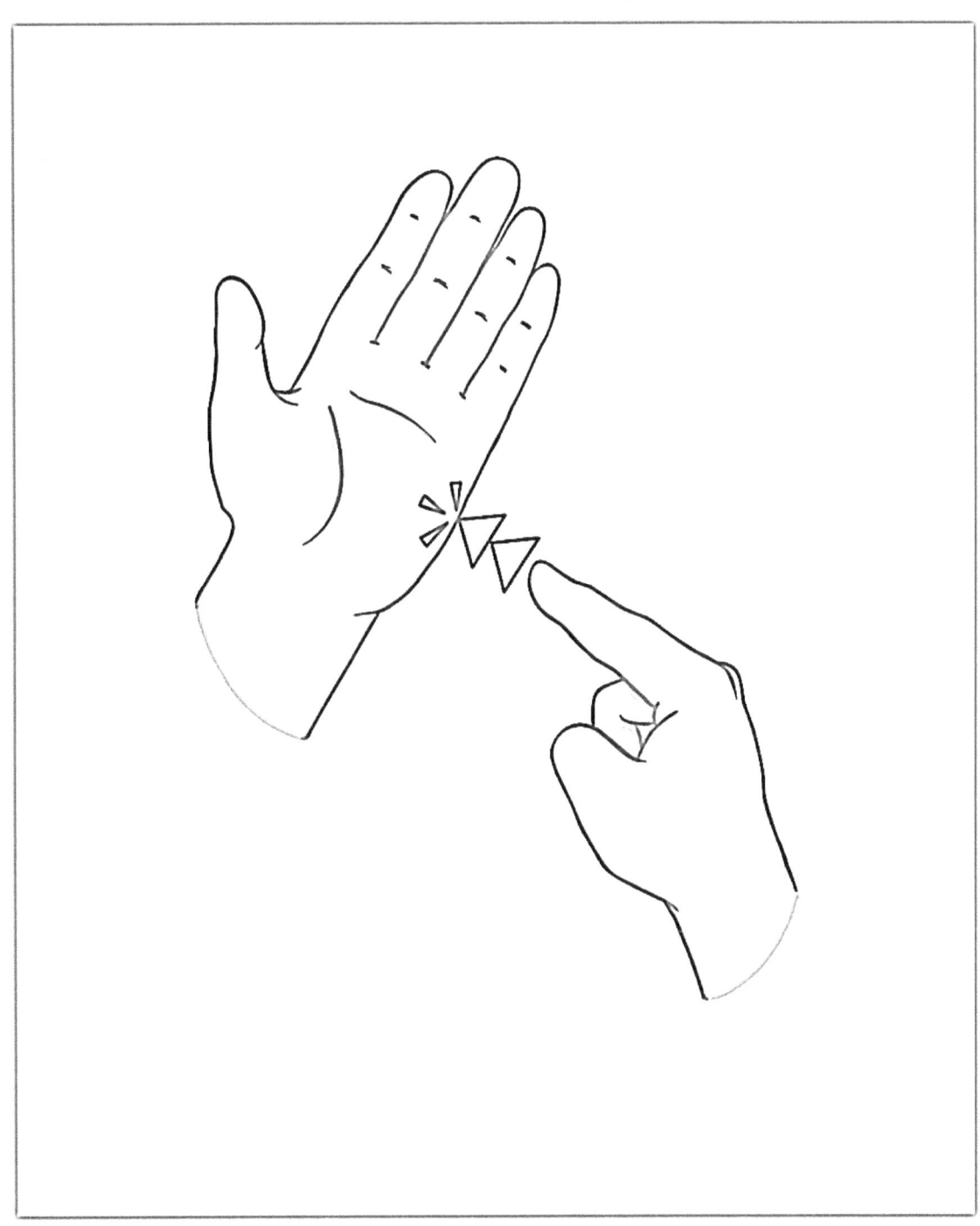

Wednesday

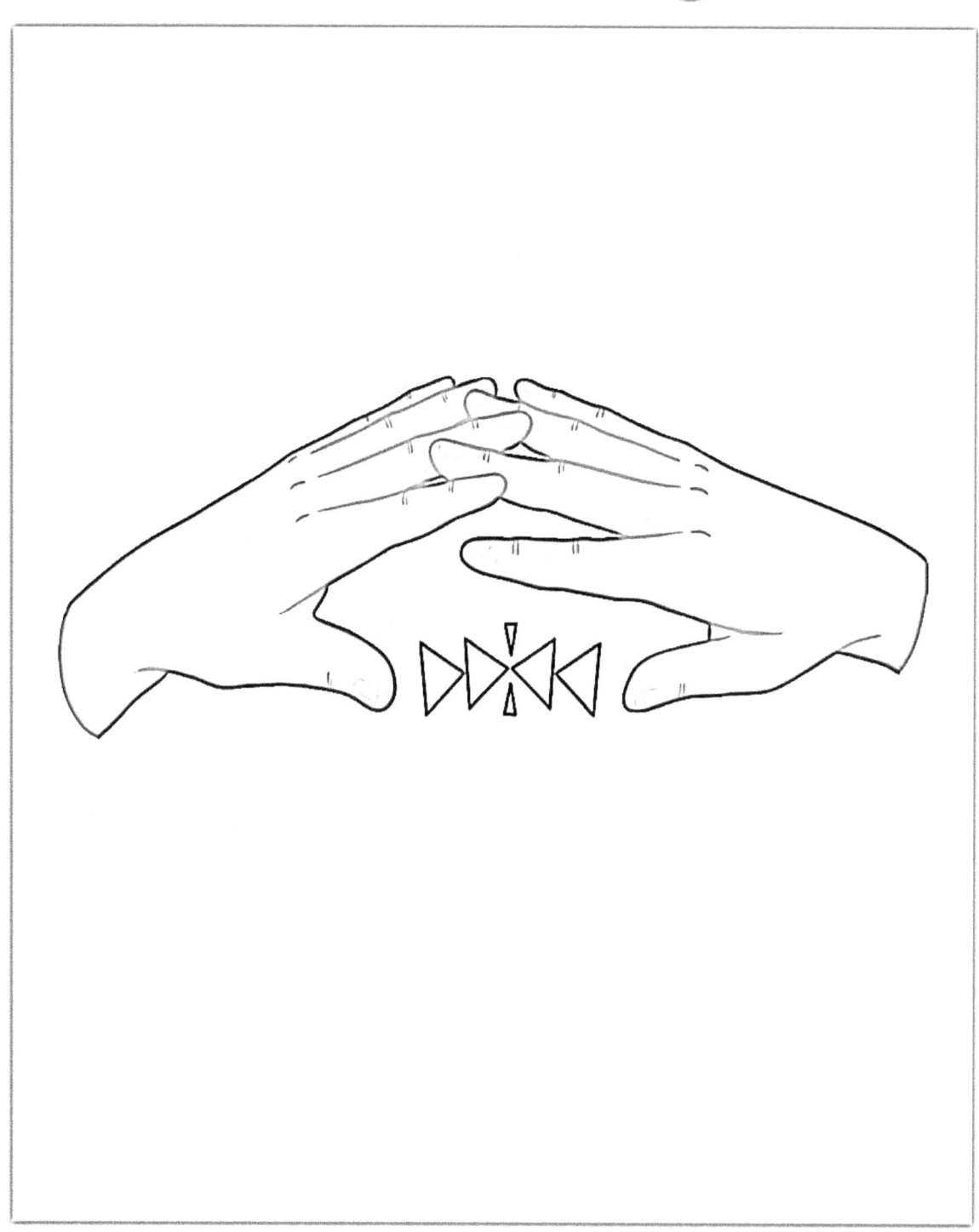

Thursday

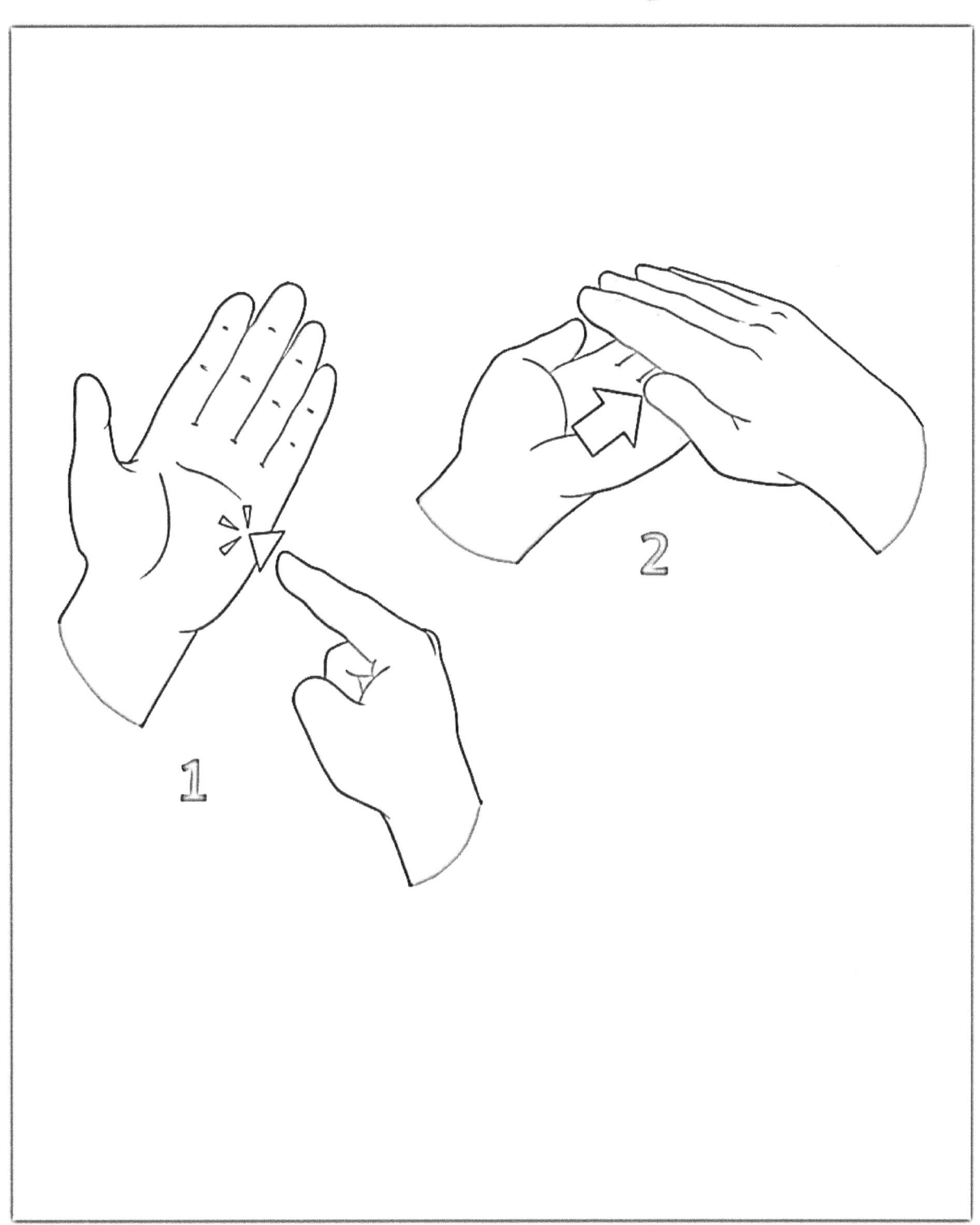

Friday

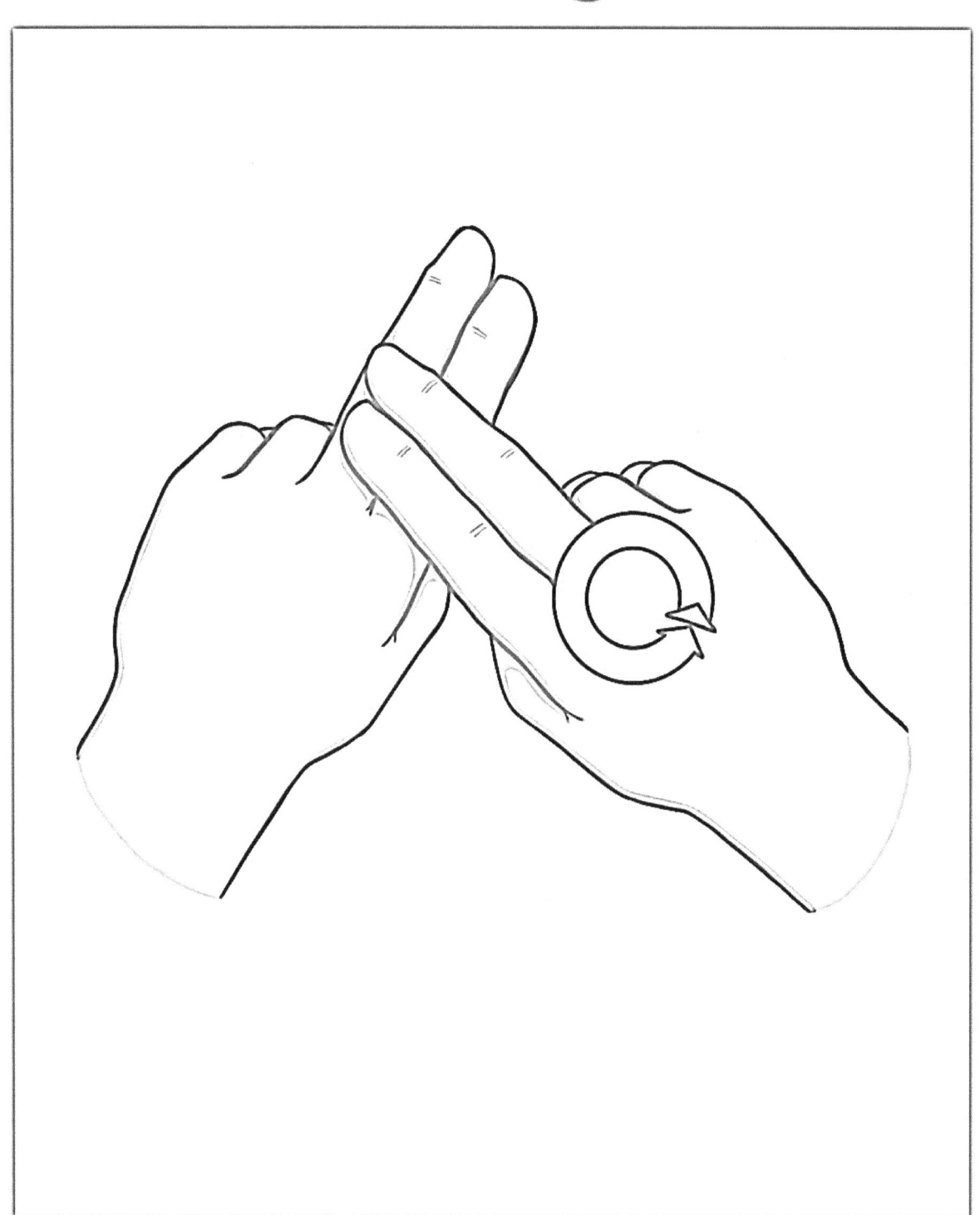

Saturday

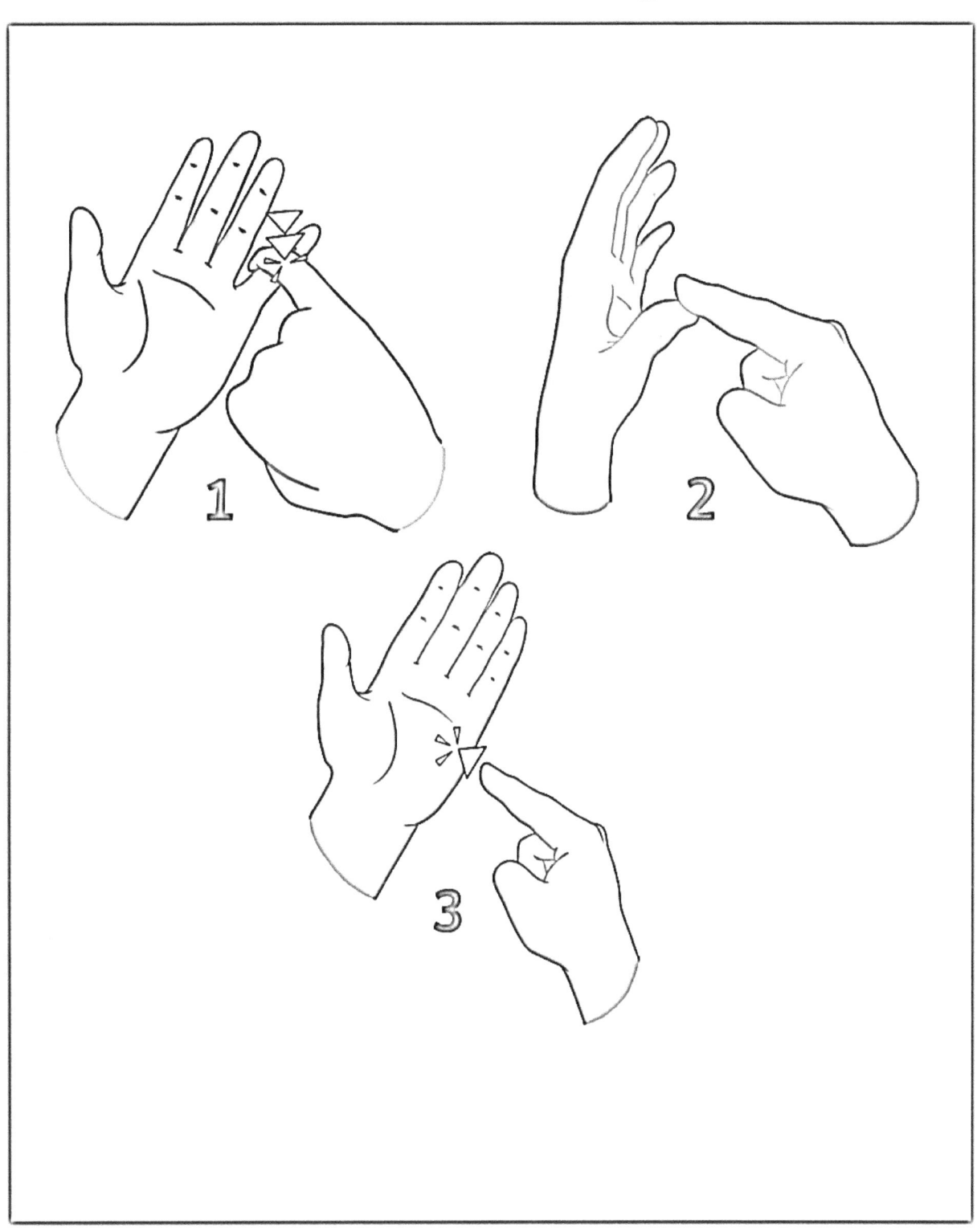

Sunday

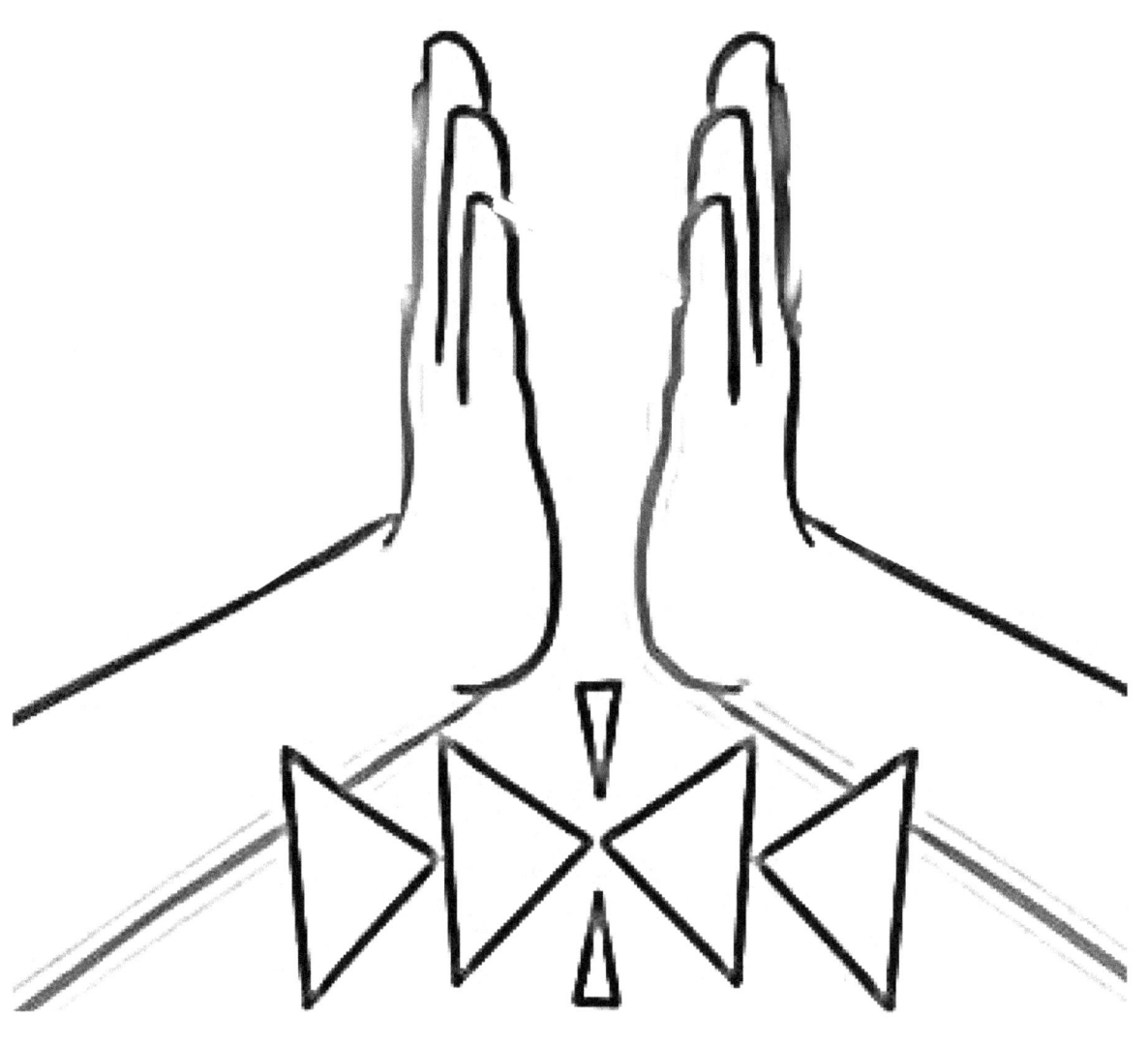

British Sign Language - Days of the Week
Matching Activity

Draw a line to match the correct sign to each day of the week

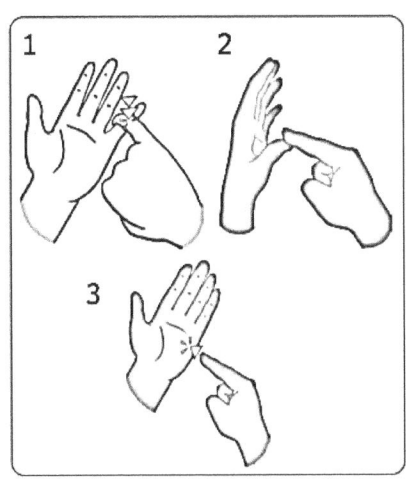
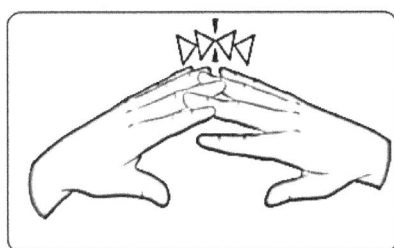

Monday

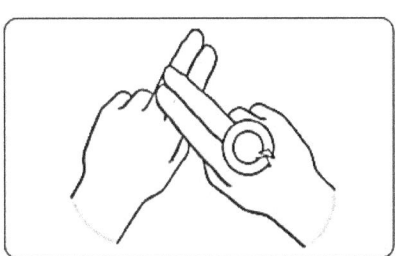

Tuesday

Wednesday

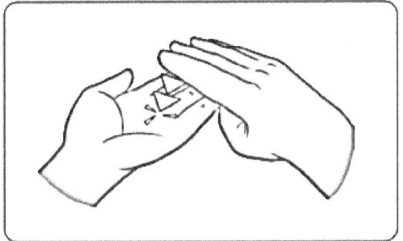

Thursday

Friday

Saturday

Sunday

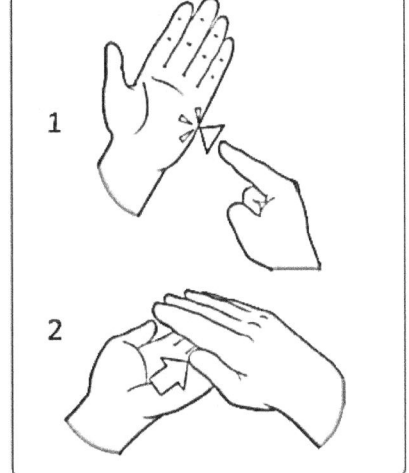
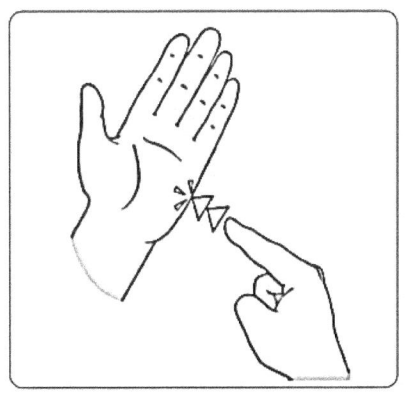

British Sign Language - Days of the Week
Matching Activity Answers

Draw a line to match the correct sign to each day of the week

January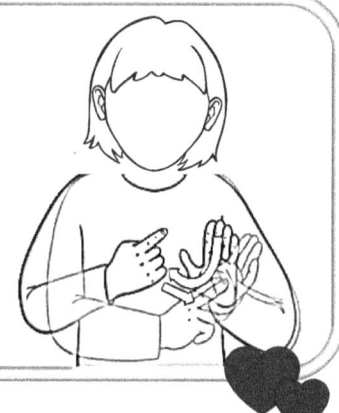

February

March

April

May

June

July

August

September

October

November

December

THANK YOU!
PLEASE LEAVE A REVIEW.

www.ingramcontent.com/pod-product-compliance
Lightning Source LLC
LaVergne TN
LVHW060220080526
838202LV00052B/4308